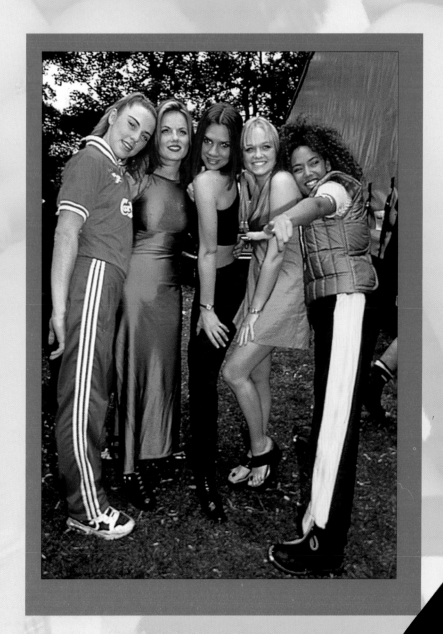

Conte

© 1997 Grandreams Limited

Published by
Grandreams Limited
435-437 Edgware Road, Little Venice,
London W2 1TH.

Written by:
Teresa Maughan, Mick St. Michael, and
Ian Welch.
Designed by Simon Joslin.

Printed in Belgium.

n t s

Introducing...

They said it was the era of the boy band...until five young ladies came along and turned pop upside-down! Instead of dressing up in a stage uniform, harmonising sweetly and smiling for the camera, these fresh new faces on the scene were clearly taking no-one's orders but their own. Each one dressed differently, acted individually, wrote their own songs and sang them their own way...with devastating results.

Suddenly only one question was on everyone's lips – so what did we want, did we really, *really* want? The answer was obvious! We just couldn't get enough of Emma, Victoria, Geri and the two Mels...and fortunately they felt the same. But this pop-star lark was all going to be on their own terms, as radio and TV interviewers found to their cost. No-one was safe, and there was nowhere for unbelievers to hide – even the gents' loo at *Top Of The Pops* was invaded as this new group took over!

And 'Wannabe' was only the start of it... Fuelling their success with amazing videos and irrepressible behaviour, the famous five followed up with three more chart-toppers in quick succession: 'Say You'll Be There', '2 Become 1' (the Christmas hit of the year) and 'Mama'. There was so much to look forward to as they travelled the world turning the globe on to their music – a message that had truly international appeal.

Despite their worldwide success, few people knew more about the group than their different images: Scary, Sporty, Posh, Ginger and Baby. But dig deeper and you'll find each has a different tale to tell of how they made it – and, now they've got together, their own perspective on the overnight fame and fortune they enjoy.

In the pages of this special, you'll find the whole story of who they are, how they got there and what they did next...as well as taking a lighthearted look into their future via the science of astrology.

If the success story keeps going strong (and why not?), look forward to a lot of stargazing in 1998!

Take five

If you've never heard of these pop sensations, you're either reading this from the comfort of your spaceship on Mars or you're a Himalayan yak farmer! Either way you're probably the only one on the planet, sorry universe, that hasn't heard of the biggest explosion of pop energy this century. But how do five ordinary people go from complete nobodies to humongous pop stars overnight? With truckloads of hard work and bags of determination, actually...

One minute you're serving mushy peas at the local chippy, the next you're eating at the swankiest restaurants, brushing bods with the rich and glam and swarming with paparazzi as soon as you so much as pick yer nose! It may sound as far fetched as an X-File but this story's for real! That's exactly how they got to be the pop world's sassiest group, erm...apart from the fact that it took three years of blood, sweat and tears to get to be the huge phenomenon that they are.

So how did five perfectly normal teenagers (well, nearly normal) end up the most famous fivesome of the 1990s? They had all bumped into each other as they moved in the showbiz auditioning circuit.

Mel B and Mel C had done a show together and Victoria met Geri in the queue to audition for the film *Tank Girl*. They soon became mates and did what all teens do – shop, gossip and lark about, talking constantly about their dreams of being successful stars.

They thought about forming a group, then started to make plans to turn words into actions. They were determined to get it right, so took things slowly. They saw an ad in *The Stage* for five females who could sing and dance, replied and were selected to be bundled down to live in a house with their new manager.

Now the fun started. After a bit of bonding, they started working on some routines and

melodies – only to discover their manager had his own plans. They claim he wanted to turn them into his idea of a perfectly formed group in the same vein as all those 'manufactured' boy groups. But these foxy chicks had got other ideas and promptly dumped him as fast as you can say 'Wannabe'.

From that point on, they decided nobody was going to tell them what to wear, eat, do or say – and they certainly weren't going to tell them what to sing! So they began to write their own songs, the first giving them their name. A demo tape happened to land in the lap of Simon Fuller (Annie Lennox's hotshot manager), and with a

mob of five fame-hungry females breathing down his neck he agreed to find them a record deal. Simon signed them to top record company Virgin – and the rest, as they say, is history…

After signing the contract, things really started moving for the five – their first single, 'Wannabe', was released and stormed into the charts at Number 3, an amazing achievement for any pop group…let alone a completely unknown all-female one. Incredibly, the song zoomed to the top spot, making them the first British all-female group to have a Number 1 with their debut single. 'It all happened so fast. One day we were no-one and then we're beating George Michael to Number 1,' laughed Mel C.

After seven weeks as a chart-topper, 'Wannabe' stomped across the European and American airwaves to reach Number 1 in 31 countries, selling over three million copies in the process. Their second effort, 'Say You'll Be There', leapt straight in at Number 1, too, and that clinched

11

the fact that they were not a one-hit wonder – these ladies were here to stay!

But it wasn't just the music that had the nation buzzing. Their outspoken views on everything from politics to showbiz stars to sex hit the headlines too! The bolshy five had succeeded in their mission to bring their music to the world. 'We've got attitude and we're not frightened to say what we think,' they proclaimed to the nation's teenagers.

'There aren't any other bands that are like us,' explains Emma. 'We want our fans to say: "Hey, they can do it, so can we."' The famous five expounded their theories at every available opportunity – in teenage mags, on chat shows and even on the bus!

'It's like feminism but you don't have to burn your bra!' says Geri. And the message is – don't be a Wannabe! 'You can do what you want, look the way you want – as long as you believe in yourself and are comfortable the way you are.'

So, you've got the music, the philosophy and then you've got the antics – the most important thing is to have fun. 'We just see it as a great big adventure,' says Geri.

They tease other showbiz stars mercilessly. 'We just have a laugh,' says Mel B, whose outrageous antics include inviting Kula Shaker to take their shirts off and throwing cake at a live French TV audience.

Geri's had more than her share of fun too – sitting stubble-chinned Canadian Bryan Adams on her knee and asking Louise if she could borrow her tweezers for a dare. 'We never mean to offend anyone,' explains Mel C. 'We're just a bit naughty!'

Their unique appeal to both the guys and the gals in terms of their looks, attitude and style is what makes them so successful. And what's more, their music is fantastic too! The fantastic five look set to fulfil their ambition to rule the world – and have one heck of an adventure along the way!

13

MEL B FACTFILE

Full name: Melanie Janine Brown

Nickname: Scary

Date of birth: 29 May 1975

Sign of
the Zodiac: Gemini

Place of birth: Leeds

Height: 5' 5"

Colour of eyes: Brown

Early occupations:
Dancer, newspaper tele-sales and actress

Favourite saying:
'Get 'em out for the lasses!'

Favourite man:
George Clooney

Greatest fear:
Not to be able to talk or communicate with people

Favourite football team:
Leeds United – she doesn't know a lot about the
game but her dad supports them

Favourite music:
'Hip-hop', rap and jungle

Best way to win an argument:
Shout and shout and shout more...even when
they've gone!

Best chat-up line:
Forget the small talk...

Nightly ritual:
I just fall down in a comfy position anywhere!

Favourite outfit:
Red Ann Summers underwear

Person most admired:
My boyfriend

Coolest thing ever done:
Turning down MN8's G-Man

Secret of success:
Being a nutter from Leeds!

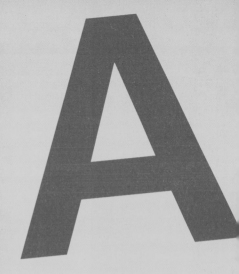

A

A is for

Attitude – and they have got plenty of that. Preaching the gospel to anyone who'll listen, and those who won't, the coolest band in the world reckon: 'We've got attitude and we're not frightened to say what we think.' Blimey!

B is for

Baby – what the rest of the group call Emma because she's the youngest. Though the others always look out for her while on tour, she's pretty handy at looking out for herself. 'They mother me,' says Emma, adding 'it's nice because I get spoilt' – but don't be fooled. Those baby-blonde candyfloss looks bely the fact she packs a karate Blue Belt punch!

C is for

Chart-toppers – Britain's hottest group stormed the charts with the release of their debut single. They knocked Gary Barlow off the top spot after 'Wannabe' shot in at Number 3. Seven weeks at numero uno and three million copies sold, they later also topped the charts in 30 more countries!

D is for

Depression – follow the ladies' prescription for the blues and you're likely to get arrested! 'If you feel depressed, just take off all your clothes and streak down the corridor. That's what we do,' advises Geri. Errr...are you *sure*?

E is for

Editors – the sassiest group on the planet caused a riot when they marched into *The Sun*'s Wapping offices and ousted Bizarre's Andy Coulson from the editor's chair. Plucky Victoria typed in her top stories despite the overwhelming pain of a trapped nerve in her shoulder.

F is for

Footy – okay, so it should be Sporty but we've already got an S with Scary! Soccer-mad Mel C is a fitness fanatic who's loopy over Liverpool. She's so famous that the club now let her into Anfield for free and Steve McManaman gets her tickets too! Sporty Mel C is always gyrating in the gym and used to do football training with the Rickmansworth ladies' team but had to stop because of all the kids turning up to watch!

G is for

Ginger – Geri Halliwell, who hails from Watford. Her mum is Spanish and wants her to settle down and get a real job...get real! Geri's got a great figure and used to model Katherine Hamnett gear.

H is for

Hair. And that can only mean Mel B! 'I'm the one with the big hair and every band needs big hair!' she says. Distinctive hair is a must for the group – Geri the fiery redhead, blonde bombshell Emma, classy cut Victoria or top knot Mel C. Each one's got her own individual look!

I is for

Independent – they may be brash and beautiful, but they're bright too. Fiercely independent, the five like being in control and calling the shots. 'We've had control of our lives from the beginning and we're not going to let that go now,' says Mel C.

J is for

Jokers. Cheeky just isn't the word. The pretty pranksters have got more front than Brighton when it comes to playing the fool. They've debagged Japanese television presenters, gatecrashed Courtney Love's room and pinched Ulrika Jonsson's bum! 'You can get away with anything as long as you're cheeky,' grins Mel B.

K is for

Kempton Kapers and we don't mean 'frolics' with *EastEnders'* Grant Mitchell (Number 6 in their top ten hunk list) either. First clues about their passion for high jinks came when the fearless five appeared at Kempton Park Racecourse and promptly climbed onto a statue of Red Rum to sing 'Wannabe' before being grappled to the ground by security. Ooo-errr!

L is for

Loudmouthed they may be, but the ferocious fivesome believe you've got to fight to be heard. 'People think we're a bunch of loud-mouths,' says Geri. 'But if you're a woman in this industry you have to shout louder than anyone else or everyone thinks you are stupid and easily manipulated – you can't win.' Or *can* you?!

M is for

Mums. Mothers are the best according to the feisty five. In fact, they are so gaga about their mummies that they recorded 'Mama' as a tribute to them. The mums starred alongside their famous daughters in the video and had a ball. 'My mum (Andrea) really enjoyed it and it was great for her to see what we do for a living,' said Mel B and Geri agreed: 'Mum (Anna) also had a fun time. It's a wonderful way to say thank you to the ones we love.' Aaaah!

N is for

Naughty. Whether it's flashing their knickers, teasing the rich and famous or posing for pics, these ladies have got a sense of fun and don't mind being wicked when the mood takes them.

O is for

Outrageous. Geri told the Backstreet Boys she had a W tattooed on each of her bum cheeks so when she bent over it spelt 'WOW'. Need we say more?!

P is for

Posh, otherwise known as Victoria, is a cool, classy chick. She's the affluent one of the group – she comes from a wealthy background in a little village in Hertfordshire and her dad runs his own business. She loves the good life – designer clothes, Gucci shoes and up-market restaurants.

Q is for

Queens – and these are definitely the Queens of Pop!

R is for

Rubbish. 'Somebody stole my rubbish!' exclaimed Geri. 'I came out of my house to see all these kids running around, then I noticed my rubbish had gone!' Spooky or what?

S is for

Scary. Mel B sets boys' knees knocking with her tough outspoken manner. 'We're not tough, we just say what we think and act on our instincts,' insists Melanie Brown from Leeds. Her mum, who's a cleaner, says Melanie's always been ambitious and the sort of person who would only do what she wanted. You don't say?

T is for

Tongues and tattoos. Body piercing and tattoos are in. Mel B's got a Japanese symbol tattooed on her tum and a ring in her tongue. Victoria had a diamond put in her fingernail, while Mel C sports a Celtic band tattooed on her arm and Geri's got a pierced tummy button.

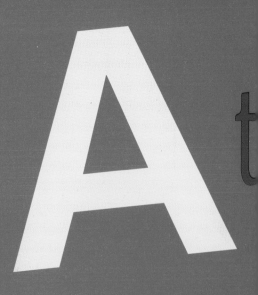

Z

U is for

USA. Britain's hottest act made pop history by scoring the highest ever chart debut position for a British act in America. They beat the bad boys of Oasis, who held the previous record of Number 21 with 'Wonderwall' last year, when 'Wannabe' stormed in at Number 11. Wicked!

V is for

Virgin are the lucky record company who signed the group shortly after they first got together. 'We're not airheads, and we run our own show,' says Emma. They have sold over a million copies of their first single 'Wannabe', making it Virgin Records' biggest selling record for 13 years. Ace!

W is for

'Wannabe' – what more need we say?

X is for

X-rated. Saucy Page 3 pictures of Ginger, taken when she was only 18, appeared in *The Sun*. The sizzling snaps of Geri posing naked against a tree and on a log were also splashed all over the paper – whose sales then went through the roof! (*Wood you believe it? – Ed*)

Y is for

Yellow-bellied, something these upfront, straight-talking lasses most definitely are *not*!

Z is for

Zig-ah-zig-ah! Have they been visited by aliens or do those words really mean something? According to them, 'Wannabe' was created in a few minutes of sitting together having a chat and a giggle – using all their favourite in phrases. And zig-ah-zig-ah is not an X-File – it's a cigar!

LIVEN UP
Your lifestyle

20

FIND A FELLA

Tired of your boyfriend? Get together with three or four pals, put their boyfriends' names on pieces of paper and drop them, folded, into a large hat. Then each draw one out. Open them together. Imagine how awful it would be to be going out with a sad specimen like that – and if that doesn't make you appreciate your fella, then chuck him!

BE WELL READ

Enrol in the local library and take out six books at random from different sections. If nothing appeals once you've got them home, try treading a page of each in turn and see if they make more sense that way. If all else fails, write your imaginary autobiography, or start your first novel on your dad's word-processor. You could be on the way to a million!

SAY IT WITH FLOWERS

Not getting enough attention from the man in your life? Send yourself flowers (or even cheaper, get a few of the little cards they come with), write passionate love notes signed with initials, and leave them lying around. Then start dropping hints that if you had more evenings out then you wouldn't be in when the phantom flower man came...

21

CATCH KELLY'S EYE

Form a group with four of your mates – or if you don't have any musical ones, put a postcard in a local shop to find some!

Buy a cheap keyboard (knew those piano lessons would come in useful sometime) and get to work learning the entire first album from cover to cover. When you've got it note-perfect, bombard Stars In Their Eyes' Matthew Kelly with pleading letters...

A MUSICAL NOTE

Have a garage sale of your old records, tapes and CDs, and use the proceeds to get some new sounds into your life. Persuade your local record shop to play something you don't know, and broaden your musical horizons. Failing that, buy your next tape or CD on the basis of the most interesting cover. If the music turns out to be awful, give it to your mum as a birthday present!

RAG TRADE

Liven up your wardrobe by dyeing your old T-shirts in up to the minute colours. Chuck out anything that's more than a year old, and absolutely refuse to wear anything you're less than 100 per cent happy with. Ask your mum or dad if they've got anything that's so old it's in again. Spraypaint old boots in colourful tones, but make sure you don't have to wear them till they're dry. If all else fails, try swapping your wardrobe with friends – a change can be as good as a rest!

BEDROOM BRILLIANCE

Redecorate your bedroom by sticking up pop posters until the boring old wallpaper disappears. For a change, plaster one corner with boy band pictures but swop their faces round to create your own groups. Replace your curtains with some really wild fabric and pin badges to the edges to create an interesting effect. Last but not least, throw away that teddy-bear duvet and replace it with something interesting – or if you can't, find something to throw over it.

WEB IT!

If your school or local library has access to the Internet, put together a home page about you and your friends. Include lots of fascinating facts, silly information and jokes, mention your immaculate taste in music and then post it on the World Wide Web.

Within days, you could have pen-friends all over the world E-mailing and asking to meet you – and wouldn't that make holidays fun!?

Full name: Emma Lee Bunton

Nickname: Baby

Date of birth: 21 January 1978

Sign of the Zodiac: Aquarius

Place of birth: London

Height: 5' 2"

Colour of eyes: Blue

Early occupations:
Child model, dancer, singer and actress

Favourite saying:
'Home is where the heart is!'

Favourite fictional hero:
Penelope Pitstop

Favourite man:
Johnny Depp or George Clooney

Greatest fear:
Prison and loneliness

Favourite football team:
Tottenham Hotspur – all her family are Spurs fans and a relation's ashes are buried at White Hart Lane

Favourite music:
Garage and house

Best way to win an argument:
I shed a tear for sympathy!

Best chat-up line:
Would you like one of my Bon Bons?

Nightly ritual:
I have that last-minute cuddle with whoever is next to me!

Person most admired:
My mum

Secret of success:
Smiling sweetly and getting away with murder!

Coolest thing ever done:
Asking rock band AC/DC who they were

EMMA
FACTFILE

20TH

you didn't know abou

Tell us something we don't know.

Okay then!

1 While on hols with Mel B in Sri Lanka, Geri handcuffed a nightclub owner to a tree because he wanted to shut the club at midnight – and left him there!

2 Emma's mum Pauline is a karate black belt and teaches children the martial art at her club, Gojukai Karate. Daughter Emma has reached blue belt, the fifth grade of nine, and Pauline has also trained all the group members, giving them lessons on how to look after themselves.

INGS
pop's hottest group

3 In the early days, the group used to be so poor they stole toilet paper from restaurants! (*What a rip-off – Ed*)

4 Mel B's mum once begged her to quit the group when it started. Andrea Brown admitted, 'I used to say she should leave because they were broke, but thank God they stuck together.' She also sends Mel B clumps of hair from her pet dog Georgia because she misses her. Weird!

5 *ER* actor George Clooney is top of their Hot Hunks top ten list, along with Denzel Washington, Bruce Willis, Ross Kemp – and, finally, newsreader Trevor McDonald. Bong!

6 The feisty five were offered £1,000,000 by the Fantasy TV Channel to strip off. 'We are being serious. Our viewers voted them the people they would most like to see naked,' said a channel spokesman. The group, of course, declined – though Geri has already bared all in saucy photo sessions when she was an unknown 18 year old which have since appeared on Page 3 of *The Sun*.

7 Mel B describes herself as 'the coolest Black Widow spider in the jungle'. Wow!

8 Emma is Prince William's favourite group member. He has pin-ups of them on his bedroom wall, with Ms Bunton in pride of place. Queen Emma? Ya never know!

9 The cheeky quintet have been thrown out of a restaurant in a casino for having a food fight. They also debagged two Japanese television presenters live on TV (*Ah so! – cheeky Ed*).

10 Geri has been voted the sexiest member of the band. A whopping 30.4 per cent of a poll taken for *Sky* magazine voted her as having a 'great personality…or pair of them!'.

11 The group once posed as friends of former 'wild child' actress Amanda De Cadenet and blagged their way into Courtney Love's (aka Mrs Kurt Cobain) hotel room. 'She made us drink tea and we watched that movie *Congo*,' they said, clearly impressed.

12 Victoria once flashed her knickers at a group of poncy business execs to give them a shock!

15 Mel C has got a long lost half-sister who she didn't know existed! Emma Williams is 15 and recognised the resemblance of her and Mel C when she saw her in publicity pics. 'To find out you've got a big sister is fantastic…but it's twice as nice to find out she is a pop star,' said Emma.

13 Geri is a direct descendant of Prince Pedro Hidalgo of Cordoba (*Who he? – Ed*) who single-handedly killed ten Moorish sentries in the 14th century. Her mother is Spanish and when she was young she used to go to bullfights. Her Aunt Maria recalls, 'Geri used to cry when the bull was killed. She always wanted us to take it home with us to save it.' Imagine having a bull in your living room…

14 Mel C's stepdad played in a band with the Beatles.

16 Cable channel The Box played 'Wannabe' no fewer than 70 times the week before the single was released. Don't touch that dial!

17 Mel B used to earn £3 an hour dancing in a bikini in the Yel Club in her hometown of Leeds. In 1992 she came top in a local beauty contest for the *Leeds Weekly News* and won a Renault Clio, a weekend in Paris for two and a place on a modelling course.

18 Emma once did a streak across a hotel lobby in Germany with Geri – the most outrageous thing she's ever done.

20 Victoria's mum has a scrapbook of cuttings 'the size of a house' on Peter André. All she needs now is Mum André's address so she can send them to her!

19 When Geri was on *Top Of The Pops* she picked up rough-hewn Canadian rocker Bryan Adams, sat him on her knee and said, 'Aren't you a lovely little boy?' Blimey!

FIVE

In the studio

In a world dominated by boy bands and cover versions, these pop sensations have blown a much-needed and very original breath of fresh air into the proceedings. As Geri insists, 'We're not some management-led concept – we call the shots. We all sing, we all dance, we all write the songs and decide on the arrangements and the way we present ourselves.'

The multi-talented fivesome started writing songs and recording demos together as long ago as 1993, at the house they then shared. It was then that they realised that emphasising the differences between them would be more interesting than becoming, as Mel C puts it, 'one of those teen acts who all wear the same clothes and do the same dance moves.'

The girls' individual musical tastes are as different as their personalities. Mel B likes rap, 'hip-hop' and jungle, while Emma favours chart pop and garage. Geri is a bit of a rock chick, admitting to liking Oasis, while Victoria favours soul with a gospel influence – Anita Baker and Toni Braxton for preference. And that was always going to come over in the music.

With typical street savvy, they signed up with a music publisher long before they looked for a record deal, by borrowing money from their parents and hiring Nomis Studios in West London in November 1994. 'About 20 publishers came along to our showcase,' Emma reveals, 'and we waited to see who could give us the deal which would suit us.'

They had the songs, and the style. With a publishing deal with Windswept Pacific under their belts, the group linked up with manager Simon Fuller – a man 'who understood that we wanted a say in how our careers would go,' (Mel B) – and the rest, as explained elsewhere, was history. It was time to cut their first record.

But studio time costs money in this hi-tech, high-pressure age, and Virgin Records suggested the girls got together with two very successful recording teams to ease their path. First was Richard Stannard and Matt Rowe, who'd worked with the likes of East 17 and PJ and Duncan. They hit it off with the

group, and worked on four key cuts on the first album, including the singles 'Wannabe', '2 Become 1' and 'Mama'.

Though much of the recording was hi-tech in the extreme, the strings used on 'Mama' and '2 Become 1' were very real. A sample of Digital Underground's 'Humpty Dance' found its way into 'If U Can't Dance' to liven up the proceedings – but as ever the ideas, words and influences were very much the singers' prerogative.

The other side of the coin was supplied by the street-sussed Absolute team, who produced the album's other six tracks including the slinky soul groove of 'Say You'll Be There'. The harmonica on that hit, fact fans, was supplied by veteran Judd Lander, whose talents graced Culture Club's 1983 chart-topper 'Karma Chameleon'!

After all this it was little surprise that Absolute, along with Stannard and Rowe, found themselves nominated in 1997 for a Brit Award in the Best British Producer category – proof positive that the studio magic that created the first album had been recognised by the music business. As ever, the famous five had it taped!

FILE

Full name: Geri Estelle Halliwell

Nickname: Ginger

Date of birth: 6 August 1972

Sign of
the Zodiac: Leo

Place of birth: Watford

Height: 5' 2"

Colour of eyes: Blue

Early occupations:
Presenter on Turkish TV, dancer, aerobics
instructor, barmaid and model

Favourite saying:
'This is what we're going to do…!'

Would like to be
reincarnated as:
Queen, a bank robber or Mother Theresa

Favourite men:
Noel Gallagher and Gary Porter (Watford
midfielder)

Favourite football team:
Watford – her home-town team

Favourite music:
All sorts – especially rock

Best way to win an
argument:
Throw in a few big words and a lot of verbal to
confuse the situation!

Best chat-up line:
Here's 10p…call your mum 'cos you're not
going home tonight!

Nightly ritual:
Plan the next day!

Person most admired:
The Fonz from *Happy Days*

Coolest thing ever done:
Feeding the homeless in cardboard city

Favourite outfit:
My birthday suit!

You don't

'We were fascinated and very pleased to hear of their political views. They're go-ahead people and we are a go-ahead party.'
Conservative Central Office

'Being in the group hasn't changed Emma a bit– she's still down to earth and normal. All five are lovely and still come round to the house. They are really good friends.'
Pauline Bunton (Emma's mum)

'Just because they like Margaret Thatcher won't stop Tony Blair liking their music.'
Labour Party HQ

'They can pack more punch than Frank Bruno and are hotter than a vindaloo curry!'
BBC's *Food And Drink*...er, *Live And Kicking*!

'They said Margaret Thatcher was the sixth member. Margaret Thatcher did her best to mess up the country...'
Pulp's Jarvis Cocker

'Blimey! Who are they?'
***Smash Hits* staff after the (then unsigned) group came unannounced into their office for a bit of a singsong**

'If my boyfriend were having an affair with one of them, I'd get back at him by having a fling with her too!'
Sexy singer Gabrielle (According to *The Sun*)

say?!

say ?!

'They are the best pop group in the world…ever.'
New Musical Express **writer Mark Sutherland**

'Mel loves being in the band and 's great to see her on telly. I'm 'ery proud of her and how hard she's worked over the years.'
Andrea Brown (Mel B's mum)

'It's incredible. We haven't seen a pop act sell this fast since Take That. It's hard to see how they can fail.'
HMV record shops after 'Wannabe' sells out

'I'd only met her for a few minutes that night but I couldn't stop thinking about her…she was very attractive, had a great figure and was confident and outgoing.'
First love Steve Mulrain on Mel B

'Even at the age of 11 she was mad about performing. She loved dancing and I'm not surprised she's done well.'
Emma Comolli, schoolchum of Victoria

'She was a natural – very attractive with beautiful eyes. She was chatty and relaxed and didn't bat an eyelid about stripping.'
The photographer who took those naughty shots of Geri, 18

'Whether they were a salesman's canny confection or a spontaneous burst, they were certainly popular. And whether they were an essay in new-age feminism or simply big fun for teenies, they were everywhere you turned an ear.'
Mail On Sunday's **review of 1996**

Just for THE RECORD

FACTS BEHIND THE WAXINGS THAT PUT THESE POP SENSATIONS ON THE MAP

'WANNABE'
RELEASED JULY 1996
HIGHEST UK CHART POSITION: 1

The summer hit of '96, this wasn't just their first ever single – it reached Number 1 in less time than it takes to apply your nail varnish! By the end of July 'Wannabe' had gone gold (400,000) after just two weeks in the charts. Then along came ex-Take That member Robbie Williams with his solo debut, 'Freedom' – but they held firm. Almost unbelievably, their fourth week at the top saw sales of 145,000. By week five, they had sold 850,000 copies in Britain alone!

As 'Wannabe' neared the million mark along came the next challenger – blond gods Kula Shaker and their hipshakin' 'Hey Dude'. But even Crispian and his knights in shining armour couldn't shift 'em, and at the end of the week were still 25,000 behind the best sellers!

The stylish, striking video that propelled the all-singing, all-dancing group to fame was directed by the team behind the Diesel Jeans ads. Yet in this case it was only their chart competitors who got the blues...

'SAY YOU'LL BE THERE'
RELEASED OCTOBER 1996
HIGHEST UK CHART POSITION: 1

Critics who claimed the group were one-hit wonders were confounded by the success of 'Say You'll Be There'. Selling 350,000 in its first week, it was certified platinum in its month of release.

Once again, the video played a key part in promoting the song – and they took a leaf out of Madonna's book by hiring her ex-boyfriend Tony Ward as one of the supporting cast members. The poor guy was subjected to torture beyond even the Material Girl's wildest dreams, being blindfolded by a black bra as all sorts of weird and wonderful weapons flew everywhere!

Yet again, the famous five had done their bit in putting a spoke in the boy-band bandwagon, knocking Boyzone off the top spot and preventing East 17 from getting there. But even after being knocked off by gruesome twosome Robson and Jerome of *Soldier Soldier* fame, they were still celebrating their amazing sales in their two weeks at the summit!

'2 BECOME 1'
RELEASED DECEMBER 1996
HIGHEST UK CHART POSITION: 1
Another Number 1 – but this time success was that bit more special, because '2 Become 1' was the Christmas Number 1 of 1996. The group held back on releasing their third record to leave the way clear for Dunblane's 'Knocking On Heaven's Door' to reach the top before they did. 'We'd happily settle for Number 2,' they said, adding 'We don't mind about chart positions – we just want to have fun.'

The video was set in New York, picturing the group in between rushing cars and among busy crowds as they each contributed their lines in what was now becoming a trademark style. And concealed within the loving lyric was a plea for safe sex.

Various versions of the single came in special seasonal packaging with Christmas messages from the stars of the show. One format included a 'Wannabe' remix for latecomers, along with an orchestral version of the A-side for fans to sing along to – karaoke, if you like! But with the lyrics having undergone a subtle change between the album and the single version, it was hard to keep up with what the new words were...

'WHO DO YOU THINK YOU ARE'/'MAMA'
RELEASED MARCH 1997
HIGHEST UK CHART POSITION: 1
This was a double A-side that suitably came with a two-fold message. The royalties were generously donated to Red Nose Day, the much-loved national charity telethon in aid of Childline which the group had been selected to open along with Dawn French, Lenny Henry, Wonderbra star Caprice and a host of other celebs. With Mel C having recently admitted how her schooldays were ruined by bullying, the cause was one that seemed appropriate.

On the other side of the coin, 'Mama' celebrated Mother's Day and, with typical generosity, the group invited their five mums Andrea (Mel B), Anna Maria (Geri), Joan (Mel C), Jacqui (Victoria) and Pauline (Emma) to take part in shooting the video as a thank you for all they'd done. An insider claimed the mums were all 'naturals' in front of the camera – now the secret was out as to where their daughters got their talent from!

Released just a week before the big day, both single and video (a spoof game show also featuring hunky Gladiator Hunter) proved a huge success.

THE FIRST ALBUM
RELEASED NOVEMBER 1996
HIGHEST UK CHART POSITION: 1
Wannabe/Say You'll Be There/Love Thing/Last Time Lover/Mama/2 Become 1/Who Do You Think You Are/Something Kinda Funny/Naked/If U Can't Dance

What more can be said about an album that's broken sales records like they're going out of fashion? Gold in 15 countries, multi-platinum in nine and an American Number 1 to boot, it shot past the five million mark with style to spare – and as the fourth single was peeled from it, it looked set to go even higher.

Even though it was released late in the year, the album ended 1996 as the UK's fourth best seller, turning seven times platinum (two million-plus sales) by early January – which means an awful lot of people had it in their Christmas stockings. The record company claim there's never been a debut album like it...and who are we to argue?

VICTORIA FACT FILE

Full name:	Victoria Adams
Nickname:	Posh
Date of birth:	7 April 1975
Sign of the Zodiac:	Aries
Place of birth:	Hertfordshire
Height:	5' 6"
Colour of eyes:	Brown

Early occupations:
Singer and dancer

Favourite saying:
'Do it…with style!'

Favourite man:
Ray Liotta or Jack Dee

Greatest regret:
Not having a boob job

Favourite football team:
Manchester United – she knows nothing about football but manager Simon Fuller supports the Red Devils

Favourite music:
Toni Braxton, Sounds of Blackness and Anita Baker

Best way to win an argument:
I give a look that would kill, then I walk away!

Best chat-up line:
Is that a designer suit you're wearing?

Nightly ritual:
I have a full facial routine and put on my silk pyjamas!

Favourite outfit:
My underwear

Secret of success:
Looking and acting good without trying

Coolest thing ever done:
Standing up a major celebrity

SAUCY SAYINGS

When it comes to sounding off, the group aren't backwards about coming forwards. If they've got a view about something they'll mouth off about it. And if it gets them into trouble – who cares?

MEL B

Mel B, the 'Northern Nutter' from Leeds, is nicknamed Scary not just because of her attitude to men but because of that mouth. 'My mouth is my best attribute – it's big and loud!' she admits. She's never short of something to say whatever the subject and she's usually the group's mouthpiece – not that they need one since they've all got plenty of lip.

ON BOYS
'Some of us have boyfriends but men don't rule our lives. They should be like mates and they should never try and come between you and your mates. Boyfriends don't last forever but girlfriends do.'
She could have any guy she wants but when it comes to other pop stars she says, 'We're really not into that pop boyfriend scene.'

ON LIFE
'Know what you want.'

ON HERSELF
'I like to shock so I'll come out with some really crude comments.'

ON STYLE
'The important thing is blusher. Always wear loads of blusher.'

ON MUSIC
'I'm into soul, hip-hop and jungle.'

ON KISSING
'I had my tongue pierced 'cos it enhances snogging.'

ON THE GROUP
Mel reckons they are all great mates. 'We would have made it happen no matter what.'
And being in the group? 'The fun is so infectious that five minutes with them gets you out of the rottenest moods.'

ON POLITICS
'I like the woman (Margaret Thatcher). Even if her policies were hard-headed, socialism is bad.'
'We'd back Michael Heseltine in a leadership election, not so much for his policies but because of his charisma.'

EMMA

Emma is the baby of the group and maybe just a little less confident than the others. She's the one who tends to hold back when the others are backchatting for Britain. She says, 'Maybe a couple of us will be quiet while the rest of us are being loud. We like to give each other room.'

ON BOYS

'I don't go for looks, I just go for someone who makes me laugh.' And she says, 'Our ideal man would be someone like a bricklayer, builder or telephone engineer. Definitely not a showbiz star.'

ON THE GROUP

'I love being in the band because it's like being with my best mates and having a laugh every day.'
'We work 14 hours a day and it can get hard.'

ON HERSELF

'With us what you see is what you get!'
'I love the smell of candyfloss.'

ON MUSIC

'I want everyone to enjoy our music.'

ON CHEEKY CHAPPIES

'I just like a man to be natural. I like naughty boys who are a bit cheeky. But I'll give them a good spanking if they step out of line!'

ON STYLE

'I may look sweet but I wear leather underwear.'

ON LIFE

'Be strong and determined and have fun.'

ON ROCK STARS

'Liam Gallagher's got very sexy eyes...but no, I don't think so.'

ON POLITICS

'We are true Thatcherites.'

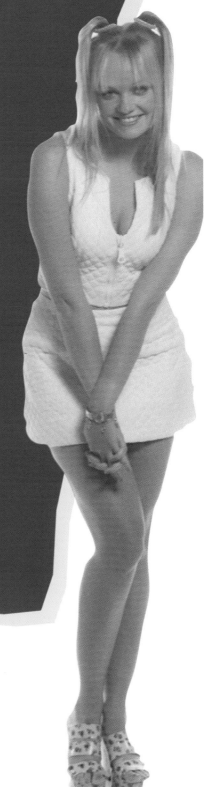

43

GERI

Geri doesn't care what she says or who she says it to! She's got an opinion on everything and is not afraid to let you know it. She describes herself as 'the spokesperson of the group.'

ON ROCK STARS
'He's (Jon Bon Jovi) not as good-looking in real life.'

ON LIFE
'Have a good attitude.'

ON HERSELF
'I'm described as the bold, mouthy one. If I was reincarnated I'd like to come back as the Queen, a bank robber or Mother Theresa.'

ON BOYS
'Boys have got to give me verbal and intellectual intercourse.'

ON DJs
'When I next see Chris Evans I'm going to snog him – just to annoy him!'

ON OASIS
'Noel Gallagher's sexy.'

ON THE GROUP
'If our record gets played in Kathy's caff in *EastEnders*, then we'll know we've made it big-time.'

ON MUSIC
'I was in the video for Nomad's "(I Wanna Give You) Devotion".'

ON POLITICS
'Lady Thatcher was the pioneer of our ideology.'

MEL C

Mel C is quite shy when it comes to the limelight and she hasn't got quite as much to say as motormouths Geri and Mel B – but when it comes to the others she's the one who shouts the orders and bosses them about!

ON HERSELF

'I'm the sporty one of the group.'
'When I was 15, I thought I was Neneh Cherry. I had my hair permed.'

ON STYLE

'If I left my house looking a mess and a photographer took my picture, I wouldn't care.'

ON THE GROUP

'I'm the minder of the band. Me and Mel B compete to see who's the hardest – we're like the Gallagher brothers.'

ON ROCK STARS

'Madonna is my heroine.'
'We couldn't believe how dinky he (Bryan Adams) was.'

ON SEX

'"2 Becomes 1" is about safe sex – an issue we feel strongly about.'

ON POLITICS

'Tony Blair is really charming.'

ON BOYS

'I'm quite shy and I find it difficult approaching guys.' But she's got some good advice when it comes to dealing with guys: 'Don't take any crap from the lads!'

ON MUSIC

'I love Tina Turner.'

VICTORIA

Victoria may talk with a posh accent but she's as capable as any of the others of producing boisterous blaring banter when she wants to.

ON LIFE

'Be happy in yourself.'

VICTORIA ON BOYS

'I do like a man who dresses well. I love Ray Liotta from *Goodfellas*.'

ON MUSIC

My heroes are Anita Baker, Toni Braxton and Sounds of Blackness.'

ON IMAGE

We don't want to be sexy, we don't want to be put up there.'

ON STYLE

She loves to shop in posh shops in London like Prada and Pollini. 'I really love designer clothes. I once spent more than £600 on a jacket.'

ON THE GROUP

'Even if nobody liked us we'd be doing this for ourselves. Having fun and being successful is a bonus.'
'I couldn't see myself doing anything else without the others.'

ON ROCK STARS

'Gary Barlow doesn't look as if he likes to have a laugh, does he?'

ON POLITICS

'John Major is a boring pillock. But he's better than the rest.'
'The good thing about Major is that because he has not got any personality he's not hiding behind a smooth facade. He can't rely on his looks, can he?'

ON HERSELF

'I used to lie and say I was taller than 5' 6".'
'I want a big house with a moat and dragons. Big dragons and a fort to keep people out.'

Five
INT

If you can make it there you'll make it anywhere...goes the chorus to 'New York New York' – and if the group hadn't been too busy singing 'Wannabe' it's a tune they could well have adopted as their own. 'Cos if 1996 had brought their breakthrough in Britain, then 1997 was the year they took the States.

With typically clever planning, the release of 'Wannabe' had been postponed to let the Christmas rush pass by. And in the silence of the post-Yule period, they made the sweetest music around. Radio stations were being inundated with phone calls every time the record was played.

The group's visit to the States was interrupted when they were asked to jet back on Concorde and declare the UK's first Wednesday night lottery well and truly open. But when it comes to having the right numbers, they had already established a winning sequence.

The Stateside release of 'Wannabe' had been followed by an unheard-of *Billboard* chart entry at Number 11 (Oasis had established the record for a British act by entering at 21 with 'Wonderwall'), followed by a leap to six – all ready for an assault on the top spot.

Next stop was Number 2, by which time they were the undisputed biggest-selling singles act in the US having sold over 700,000 copies of 'Wannabe'. With the top spot depending on radio airplay as well as sales, it was only a matter of days before the airwaves fell to their charms. With the album shipping gold (that's half a

Janet Jackson heard enough to convince her she wanted to be the sixth member. 'I've only heard "Wannabe",' she gushed, 'but it's enough to convince me they're really good. I'd love to work with them.' Talks were to take place between their respective managers – so don't be surprised if you should see an extra figure in those dance routines, your eyes may not be deceiving you!

million copies, fact fans) following its February release, nothing could have been better.

Paul Conroy, the managing director of the Virgin Records label was predictably ecstatic. 'I think America has been looking for new stars and it would be surprising if "Wannabe" hadn't worked in the US after being a success everywhere else.' He also thought it showed the way for others to follow. 'It's going to open everyone else's eyes to British music,' he grinned.

HE STATES

The group had certainly prepared the groundwork for their success, having spent ten days the previous November sussing out the lie of the land. Now the highlight of their two-week Stateside assault on 14 February was an appearance at the Gavin music-industry showcase in New Orleans where they played to a small but select audience of radio station executives.

In case any one should have overlooked the date it was Valentine's Day – and there was little doubt that someone somewhere was going to make a fortune out of producing those heart-shaped bumper stickers. Only this time they were going to read not 'I Love NY' but 'US Loves You'…

WHY AMERICA LOVES THEM

'They're the biggest phenomenon in the country – everybody's taken to them in the US!'
DAVE UNIVERSAL, KISS 98.5 RADIO, BUFFALO

'The thing about "Wannabe" is that it's short, sweet and simple. Just one listen and you know it's a smash.'
MARK REID, KQKY RADIO, NEBRASKA

'Now the album's come out it's going to be *huge*. And the second single, "Say You'll Be There", is going to be even bigger than "Wannabe".'
BRIAN STOLL, WLVY RADIO NEW YORK

'The pop sound is beginning to happen again in the US. Alternative rock has run its course and listeners are looking for a fresh, new sound.'
JOHN REYNOLDS, KHKS DALLAS

THE ULTIMATE

So how much do you know – do you really, *really* know – about the group? Try our tricky 20-question test and find out!

1. In which country did Geri host a talk show?
a) Turkey
b) England
c) Australia

2. Which part of the body has Mel B had pierced?
a) Tummy
b) Nose
c) Tongue

3. What did Victoria's mum think she was joining when she joined the group?
a) A bunch of nice, sensible people
b) A bunch of hooligans
c) A street gang

4. Who has a martial arts teacher for a mum?
a) Mel B
b) Mel C
c) Emma

5. Which football team does Sporty support?
a) Manchester United
b) Liverpool
c) Fulham

6. What is the group's record label?
a) Umbro
b) Adidas
c) Virgin

7. What did the group allegedly decide to do at *Top Of The Pops*?
a) Gatecrash the men's loos
b) Deliberately sing the wrong lyrics
c) Scare Boyzone witless

8. Which member is considered a real laydee?
a) Mel B
b) Victoria
c) Emma

48

Fan challenge

9. What is Sporty's favourite piece of clothing?
a) Her extra large Bon Jovi sweatshirt
b) Her socks
c) Her Adidas tracksuit bottoms

10. What did Emma lie about?
a) Her age
b) Her underwear size (!)
c) Her family

11. What did Mel B enjoy most about New York?
a) Riding in a yellow cab
b) Buying a real American hot dog
c) Snogging Tom Cruise (allegedly)

12. Whose mum loves all the members – except, allegedly, her own daughter?
a) Victoria
b) Mel C
c) Mel B

13. Which member gave her boyfriend a pair of hot pants?
a) Mel C
b) Victoria
c) Geri

14. What does Victoria claim she 'looks awful' without?
a) Fashion items
b) Make-up
c) Her four mates

15. Which member of the group is a secret poet?
a) Geri
b) Emma
c) Mel B

16. Who does Emma have on her bedroom wall?
a) Chris Evans
b) The Chippendales
c) The Muppets

17. Why has Geri sometimes been late for performances and TV appearances?
a) Trying to find her shoes
b) Putting money on a horse
c) In the loo

18. What does Posh have on her fingernail?
a) Nail polish
b) A little diamond
c) A tattoo

19. Where and when did Emma and Victoria first meet?
a) In a school play together when they were young
b) A public loo
c) A rave

20. Who is Sporty's dream hunk?
a) Tom Cruise
b) Bruce Willis
c) Jim 'The Mask' Carrey

How You Rated

If You Scored 1-7...
Call yourself a fan? We're not sure you'd be able to tell your Mel B from your Maggie Thatcher! Throw away those Nolan Sisters records (*Who they? – Ed*), re-read this fabulous book to the strains of a certain album and you'll feel a whole lot better about the world.

If You Scored 8-15...
Not bad...but don't get too cocky, there's still some serious room for improvement! So put on that Walkman, get swotting and you, too, could soon be a superfan. And when you get down to it, that's what we all Wannabe, isn't it?

If You Scored 16 or over...
Well, what can we say? Either you *are* one of the group (*In which case can we have your autograph, please? – Ed*) or you've followed them from the very start. Keep on keeping the faith with the famous five and we're sure you'll soon be reaping the reward.

Questions devised by Georgina Heatley

51

MELC

FACT FILE

Full name: Melanie Jayne Chisholm

Nickname: Sporty

Date of birth: 12 January 1976

Sign of
the Zodiac: Capricorn

Place of birth: Widnes

Height: 5' 6"

Colour of eyes: Hazel

Early occupations:
Singer, ballet dancer and fish'n'chippy

Favourite saying:
'You'll never walk alone!'

Would like to be
reincarnated as:
A striker for Liverpool

Favourite man:
Bruce Willis

Favourite football team:
Liverpool – and she gets into Anfield for free as
often as she can!

Favourite music:
Bruce Willis, Neneh Cherry and Madonna

Best way to win an argument:
I deck 'em!

Best chat-up line:
I've got two tickets for a Liverpool match, do you
fancy comin'?

Nightly ritual:
I do 50 stomach crunches!

Person most admired:
Steve McManaman

Coolest thing ever done:
Having our song played at Anfield

Secret of success:
Being yourself

All in the

If you're a fan of the group, you'll be no stranger to stargazing. But did you know the science of calculating and interpreting the positions of the planets has been going on for centuries? It's called astrology – and since it's thought over 25 per cent of us read the horoscope in our daily paper it's something you can't just ignore.

Sadly, Mystic Meg was unavailable to talk to us due to unforeseen commitments (*ha ha –Ed*), so we've gone ahead ourselves and sketched out a guide to pop's brightest stars, trying to find reasons why they've become the most popular group in the universe. One thing's for sure – these heavenly bodies are enough to send even Patrick Moore into orbit!

Our guide to the five individuals' fortunes is a light-hearted one – but while we've been gazing heavenward we've tried to find the good and bad points associated with each of their zodiac signs, together with a few of the real-life stars they share them with. Take a look at that information and you may just start to see them in a different light!

We've no evidence that they are astrologically inclined (though Geri's been known to moon on rare occasions), but we reckon even they may be interested in our findings.

If you share a sign with one of them, read on and see if you agree or disagree with our astrological assessment of their character. We can guarantee that, whatever your verdict, this is one (milky) way you've *never* looked at them before...

ars
GERI
LEO

GOOD POINTS
Optimistic, intelligent, loving and affectionate

BAD POINTS
Bossy, short-tempered, critical

FELLOW LEOS
Madonna, Belinda Carlisle, Pauline from *EastEnders*

As the sign of the Lion straightaway suggests, Leos are dominant characters who very much want to be kings (or queens) of the jungle. And believe us, it's a jungle out there! Geri certainly has the growl to tame most people, but friends will find under that proud exterior lurks a loving heart.

Leos are amazingly loyal to friends, they'll forgive almost anything if they value the relationship. But they expect you to know that, so don't blow a fuse when they criticise your latest look or tell you something about your lifestyle – they're only trying to help!

The extrovert sign of the zodiac is perfect for Geri, who likes to think of herself as the leader of the pack. It's certain the other four look up to her as the oldest and most experienced. And Leos rarely have regrets…so don't expect any hand-wringing about those much-exposed 'Page 3' snaps.

Leo lasses should set their sights on the signs of Aries and Sagittarius when they're looking for a mate. And though we're sure Geri's not keen on settling down just yet, we could mention the likes of Chris Evans (oops!), Jean-Claude Van Damme (oops again), Marti Pellow, Kiefer Sutherland and Luther Vandross as planetary-approved matches. She should stay away from Capricorn and Virgo men, who'd be likely to put her on a short rein – so no snogging Curly from *Coronation Street* then!

All in all, Geri's a Leo who's fun to be with. And unlike most lions you're unlikely to find her behind bars (*more likely in front of one – cheeky Ed*). Cheers!

MEL B

GEMINI

GOOD POINTS
Great company, charming and witty,
talkative

BAD POINTS
Immature, flirty, unreliable

FELLOW GEMINIS
Kylie Minogue, Nicole Kidman,
Cyndi Lauper

As with all Geminis, there are two distinct sides to Scary's character – we of course only see the extrovert one! Offstage, she can be really quite sensitive. After all, you'd not guess she writes poetry, would you? But she'll only show it to her closest friends.

If it comes to a night on the town, Mel B is definitely game. You'll never get a word in edgeways, of course, and she'll be full of her own plans while maybe you want to talk about yours. Away from the spotlight she'll be just a little different, though the chances for rest and relaxation these days are few and far between.

This star sign's favourite colour is yellow, a prime component of leopardskin and other exotic fabrics Mel favours. The lucky number for all Geminis is five – and that couldn't be better for a member of this quintet!

Just make sure you don't mention the favoured planet, Mercury…Mel's been

known to run up huge phone bills as it is! (*It's good to talk – Ed*)

When it comes to choosing a partner, Geminis are compatible with Librans and Aquarians. That gives Mel the choice of such hunky types as Declan Donnelly, Suede's Brett Anderson, East 17's Tony Mortimer or INXS's Michael Hutchence (providing she can prise Paula Yates off his manly bod!). On the other hand, we'd like to see her on a blind date with funnyman Aquarian Vic Reeves – there'd not be a dull moment with the two of them painting the town red!

Geminis are notoriously unreliable, though as a friend you may well decide being stood up on occasion is a price worth paying for the company of a really entertaining type.

AQUARIUS

GOOD POINTS
Optimistic, very friendly, talkative

BAD POINTS
Doesn't suffer fools, unromantic, forgetful

FAMOUS AQUARIANS
Michelle Gayle, Bobby Brown, Mark Owen, Robbie Williams

Aquarius is a water sign – and that suits the purest member of the group! She certainly lives up to her star sign's good points: you can't shut her up, she genuinely believes anything is possible if you put your mind to it and you won't find a better or more loyal friend this side of the known universe.

But to someone who doesn't know them Aquarians can appear cool, hard and sometimes uncaring. They're not the types to wear their heart on their sleeves, and personal matters are likely to stay just that – personal. Emma's not comfortable with the glare of the media spotlight, but she knows she's got to live with it.

The compatible signs for Aquarians to look out for are Libra and Gemini, two of the more tolerant groups in the astrological system. There's plenty of choice when it comes to the heavenly twins: footballer Paul 'Gazza' Gascoigne, enigmatic Prince (the artist formerly known as, Symbol, or whatever he's calling himself today), Mick Hucknall, Johnny Depp, Michael J Fox...the list is endless. On the other hand, cute l'il Emma might want to consider a father figure like Sir Cliff Richard – that legendary Bachelor Boy who's surely the most eligible Libran around!

Aquarians are the thinking sign of the zodiac, and Emma's someone who's rarely likely to be lost for a thought or comment. She cares for the planet in general and the environment, and hasn't got so caught up in the rock'n'roll lifestyle that she's forgotten what makes the world go round. Catch her on her own and expect a really interesting conversation – if she's got the time!

EMMA

VICTORIA

ARIES

GOOD POINTS
Generous to a fault, straight-talking, romantic

BAD POINTS
Self-centred, unreliable, impatient

FELLOW ARIES
Lisa Stansfield, Damon Albarn, Celine Dion

Surprisingly for such a stylish laydee, Victoria isn't much seen in Aries' favourite colour, red. She's just a little more sophisticated, and takes her sign's ability to spend money like it's going out of fashion to extremes when she goes shopping for designer outfits.

She likes buying gifts for others too, so mates can expect extravagant birthday presents when the royalties start coming through. This particular star sign isn't one known for salting away money in building society accounts: enjoy it while you've got it is Aries' motto.

Since her sign's lucky number is seven, we might assume that Ms Adams is planning on a large family once she settles down – or maybe it's just the number of gold discs she wants on her wall! Yet there's plenty of time for all that, as the star sign is a party-loving one. Life's too much fun to slow down yet, and we predict Victoria will still be free and single five years from now.

When it comes to romance, Aries laydeez gravitate towards Leo and Sagittarius as the only signs likely to put up with their wacky ways. Leo men include Arnie Schwarzenegger (too muscly?), Christian Slater (too small?), Steve Martin (a father figure) and veteran *Bullseye* presenter Jim Bowen (smashing!). Okay, let's try Sagittarians: Billy Idol, Gary Lineker, Ryan Giggs and Linford Christie (*that's better – Ed*).

Victoria's romantic, as those of her sign tend to be, though beware if you're a potential boyfriend – Ariens break promises like nobody's business. We suggest a ball and chain on this ram in case she finds greener fields elsewhere!

CAPRICORN

GOOD POINTS
Modest, well organised, friendly

BAD POINTS
Pessimistic, unadventurous, over-sensitive

FELLOW CAPRICORNS
Gary Barlow, Easther from Eternal, Mel Gibson

Capricorn is a star sign that suits Mel C down to the ground... Like her fellow goats, she's someone who takes life pretty seriously, and expects to be rewarded for her efforts. Well, Mel's done okay so far: let's hope she's still as happy if and when the hits are harder to come by.

Capricorns also tend to hero-worship their idols, which in Sporty's case means wearing the red and white of her fave football team. With their record of success they should keep her starry-eyed for the foreseeable future.

Astrologically speaking, Mel is someone who's well worth knowing as a friend, who never forgets a birthday and is very proud of what she and her nearest and dearest have achieved. It's always been that way ever since she was at school.

Capricorns looking for love can expect interest from Virgo and Taurus. Celebrity males born under the sign of the bull include ex-Take Thatter Howard Donald, U2's Bono, Let Loose singer Richie Wermerling and ex-*Baywatch* hunk David Charvet. If Mel doesn't fancy any of them, vivacious Virgoans a-plenty include Simon Mayo, Richard Gere, Hugh Grant (*oooh!* -Ed) and, when he finally grows up, Macaulay Culkin. We were going to mention Michael Jackson, but he was happily married at the time of writing!

Only one astrological note rings false. Capricorn's favourite shade is brown – a tad tasteful for someone who likes the bright colours and sporty stripes. Perhaps she should swap with Victoria...

MEL C

FIVE
For the future

When you've recorded the most successful debut single of all time and seen it race to the top of the chart in over 30 countries, the only way you can go is down, right? Wrong!

Far from failing to live up to the hype, the famous five have managed to keep their heads while all around them were losing theirs, zig-ah-zig-ah-ing merrily onwards in a globetrotting timetable of personal appearances that's ensured that, for the moment at least, the future's very bright indeed.

With successful singles in so many countries, the danger is of course that they might spread themselves too thinly, unable to stop other musical sensations equalling and overtaking their fame. But this is the video age – and just as their cable TV appearances captivated a large part of Britain and ensured 'Wannabe' got off to a flying start, so the clips that have entertained fans on the release of each and every single will play a part in keeping them up there where they belong in all corners of the known pop world.

As landmark after landmark falls to their charms, the group are left with fewer goals to aim for. Turning on the Oxford Street Christmas lights? Done that! American Number 1 single and album? Yeah… Double Brit Award winners? Yawn. Could success lose some of its sparkle for our lovely laydeez?

Not if Geri has a say – and when *doesn't* she? 'I've been banging on the door since I was 16,' she explains, 'and I've waited a long time for this. That's why we're not gonna get carried away…'

And if their style is something the group cooked up themselves, they're not likely to be blown off course by expensive stylists and the like. 'We don't really like anything they've brought for us to wear,' whispered Emma as they hit New York for their first magazine cover story, 'so we're going to wear our own stuff!' As long as they refuse to be bullied and continue playing the fame game their way, they should be alright!

As for the day when the hits fade (*never! – Ed*), Geri's already tried a few careers such as gameshow hostess, so there should be no shortage of offers from the gogglebox. How about giving them their own show? Failing that, they could always move into politics: after their last pronouncements, Conservative and Labour MPs were quick to offer support.

Then there's Hollywood, which even now is cooking up movie ideas for them to star in. They'd be naturals for a cartoon series, while we reckon next time James Bond dons his dinner jacket Scary would make an ideal opponent – with no shortage of potential Bond fillies elsewhere in the ranks. 'Is that a pistol in your pocket, Mr Bond, or…' (*cut! cut! – Ed*).

For Mel B, though, the long-term future (if she's good) means heaven: 'An ideal world where there'd be no power trips and no money because everything you need would be there. Everyone would be good-natured.' But heaven's gotta wait – 'cos the group are too busy bringing us their version of pop paradise. Long may they reign!

61